As If I Knew What I Was Talking About

Sam Buck

Table of Contents

Dedication

This book is dedicated to my grandchildren and to those who are seeking a more tangible means of experiencing some very basic truths they sense will lead towards a happier and more fulfilling life.

I was very fortunate to inherit much of what I am sharing. The balance has come from teachers, mentors, and my direct experiences.

I feel so grateful for what I have, that I wanted to share my fortune with others.

So… this book is dedicated to you.

Acknowledgments

Are you suffering physically, mentally, emotionally, or spiritually? Almost certainly the answer is yes to one or more of those aspects of our lives.

I am a very empathetic person who felt compelled to share information that I believe will enhance the quality of life of those who are consciously or subconsciously longing and ready to receive what I have to offer.

I've gained tremendous insights through the gifts of living through; the death of my oldest son at 33 by his own hand with no signs of depression, my youngest son suffering from and then making a major recovery from schizophrenic type circumstances, surviving late stage 4 cancer twice, major financial setbacks, and moving past thoughts of divorce to deep abiding love through most of our 44 years together.

Like anyone sharing anything, my words are a synthesis of what I've been able to absorb and now translate into an expression that I am hoping you can relate to. Did your questions created the void nature sought to fill through inspiring me to share in this way?

There are so many who I've benefited from that I would need many pages of fine print to document.

I am fortunate in that the core influence has been through my parents and the rest of my lineage including my aunt gifting me the book Jonathan Livingston Seagull when I was 18 and hungry for such insights.

The most current gifts of influence have been through, Rupert Sheldrake, Bruce Lipton, Steve Greer, and Dr. Joe Dispenza. All stand on the shoulders of many others and each are making huge contributions to life as we know it. Dr. Dispenza is changing the world in the most dramatic way, as are people who share their NDE's (near-death experiences). Expand yourself by accessing any of these via YouTube. Do so and my mission is accomplished.

About The Author

Sam Buck lives on San Juan Island in Washington State where he was raised and has loved living for 53 of his 70 years. From age 12, he lived on a 210-acre waterfront farm, feeding cattle, riding horses, and all that entails. As a young man, he ran heavy equipment, became a commercial fisherman, and then became a co-owner/operator of a restaurant, followed by becoming a practitioner and teacher of energy work called Polarity Therapy. He then worked as a network marketer, and finally ending up being a realtor for 34 years.

Sam has been a seeker of spiritual truth since early high school, which drew him to explore many pathways. Sam has been married for 44 years. He and his wife Jane were blessed with two boys and two grandchildren, and all are vegetarian by choice rather than being coerced.

Life led Sam to study NDE's (near-death experiences) providing profound insights to living life that were critical to surviving the suicide of their oldest 33 year old son John. There were zero indications to them or any of his friends that such was even possible. The depth of pain is only known by those who have suffered in a similar way and yet, as hard as it might be to conceive of, Sam says wonderful expansions of awareness and connection happened as a result of his passing. He said, all life events are gifts for the sake of the soul's growth.

Sam grew up dyslexic but did not know so until he was 34, when it was mostly corrected through the work of Dr. Bruce Dew's understanding of educational kinesiology. The moment he fluently read a paragraph in reverse for the first time, he immediately said, oh my God, this is why people like to read! All the guilt he felt for the lack of academic achievement immediately disappeared.

Being forced to solve traditional problems outside of the well-traveled pathways, is one of the many gifts of dyslexia.

AS IF I KNEW WHAT I WAS TALKING ABOUT

Is this booklet a lead into religion? No.

Are there some references of a spiritual nature? Yes.

Any dogma? Nope.

The words of this publication are meant to be straightforward with little effort towards "correct etiquette". If you picked this booklet up, any words you read are meant for you for many reasons. It may be to affirm a positive or negative perspective, open or close a door, or provide helpful insight. Whatever the case may be, a purpose has been served for you at this moment in your life.

If your thirst to know more about this life you are living is yet to be quenched, read on, my friend.

Subjects:

1) Relief for emotional, mental, and spiritual pain.

2) Relief from any source of discomfort, including fear, anxiety, sadness, apathy, anger etc.

3) How to gain joy, peace, love, purpose, and deep connection.

Subjects 1 & 2 above have one basic cause: the friction we experience when we disconnected from and resisting going with the flow of the river of our life.

Is the fundamental background noise in your head constantly declaring, "I want things to be different than they are"?

Whether stated or not, much too often, most of us are essentially whining and complaining to the source from which we came that we are unhappy because they, he, she, someone, or something, got it wrong! Whoever is in charge screwed up and has not been giving me what I want.

What would you think of a child at their birthday party standing in the middle of a bunch of opened and unopened gifts, complaining about not having more? You might judge that child as spoiled, undeserving, or something along those lines.

Have you been complaining, when upon further examination, you actually have much to be grateful for?

My goal is not to chastise or try to create a feeling of guilt or shame for you or anyone else. A fresh perspective is my only goal.

We have all experienced a moment in which we said, "I've never thought of it that way,"

Can you sense a kernel of truth in the following?

The source of our being compels us to recognize that every experience leads towards a greater consciousness for us and for all who witness our behavior at any given moment.

Are you a random event within a world of accidents, or are you here "with a purpose"?

Is there a point to the occasional or constant chaos that we witness?

There is very compelling non-religion-based evidence available that I will share with you shortly, which may affirm that there is most definitely a beautiful purpose to all that unfolds before us.

If, by studying some of this evidence, your entire perception of what this life experience is about became more beautifully tangible, would that time have been well spent?

Every day you are being showered with gifts, and all that is needed to experience them is to refocus your attention from the pain of disappointment to appreciating what you have. Recent science has confirmed that every time you make that shift, you change your body's chemistry in a way that dramatically improves your quality of life more than almost anything else you will ever do.

When experiencing disappointment or some form of depression, if you become conscious enough to think about even a very insignificant attribute you can appreciate, you will immediately think of a second, third, fourth, etc. Doing so lifts you up, and from that higher perspective, it is easier to see your way forward. (I know from personal experience that if you integrate the simplicity of what I have just shared, your life will improve.)

While in such a deep state of depression due to financial failure, I was so depressed that I had to consciously tell myself to inhale. Fortunately, I heard a little voice in my head say, "Think of something, anything that you can appreciate. Even though it sounds silly, I realized I could appreciate that I had a little toe, because not everyone has one. Then I realized I had two, then all my toes, my feet, my legs, and a healthy body with which to start over again. Within moments, I was feeling much better. Over the years, I've implemented that same strategy many times, which always creates immediate relief.

How can you "know" with no doubts that life's unfolding is happening <u>for you</u> instead of <u>to you</u>?

Science still cannot tell us how gravity works, yet we have so much evidence that we accept it exists.

The following few sentences might change your life, so stick with it for at least a few more paragraphs. For just a few moments, suspend past conclusions and open your skeptic's filter (we all have one) enough to consider some new possibilities.

According to research, about 4% of us have some sort of a Near-Death Experience or NDE.

An NDE is an event in someone's life in which, most commonly, they are pronounced physically dead and yet they experience going up through a tunnel into spectacular light and love. While there, they meet and interact with loved ones who have previously passed on and/or other spiritual beings and are then returned to this earthly existence. They are generally told, "It is not your time yet", "You have more to do before you can come to stay", or something to that effect.

These events happen across all levels of society, and even if it was only 2%, that still equates to 200 out of every 10,000 people. Most of those who experience them had never heard of one before due to the fact that most of those who have had one don't talk about them out of fear of ridicule.

Atheists are no longer atheists, and while religious people still appreciate their religion, they become less religious and more spiritual. Each now understands that all paths and religions have their purpose despite what they now understand to be the many human distortions of the truth that have become religious dogma.

When one experiences an NDE, their life is changed in a very profound and positive way.

The two most common attributes for those who have had an NDE are:

1) They are liberated from the fear of death. They experienced that <u>who they know themselves to be, does not end</u>. They also experience that life is a beautiful continuum and now know that when they have fully served their purpose for being here, they will return to their true home and continue to grow there.

2) Some have "life reviews" in which they re-experience the entirety of their life's journey, including – and this is very important – experiencing what others experienced from them,

be it pleasant or unpleasant. No one is there to pass judgment upon them. They simply understand how, at certain junctures of their life, they could have made better decisions while at the same time understanding that even so, there is always a positive and necessary purpose for everything that happens.

They now understand with great certainty that life is not just a bunch of random events of bumping into this and that. They witnessed a positive purpose for all they experienced and those who were impacted, to one degree or another, by either their actions or inactions. They now live in trust that such is always the case, so they no longer linger in the old patterns of seeing the world through "victim, winner-loser" consciousness.

They now understand that just like the pain of repetitively lifting weights to grow one's muscles, the pain and suffering caused by mental, emotional, and spiritual challenges is a means towards growing those muscles. They also witness that "going with the flow", so to speak, causes joy, peace, and a sense of purpose, which grows our ability to make better choices, entraining us towards a more illuminated state of being.

Their NDE taught them to accept and trust that whatever is around the next bend will be <u>for</u> their benefit and <u>for</u> the benefit of all. That trust is not based on blind faith. For them, it is now a known truth, based on what they personally witnessed.

With those truths firmly in place, they walk through the rest of their lives with much greater peace in their hearts than most of us. Is it possible for you to gain that knowledge without dying and coming back? Yes!

As previously mentioned, based on others' research, as many as 4% of us have had an NDE to a greater or lesser degree. That is 40,000 per million, not one in a million. You probably know someone who has had a similarly profound experience, but like most, have chosen to keep it private because of the fear of losing credibility.

How can you gain exposure to these people? For a good reason, your mind will not accept my words on their own. It is only through repetition of fairly consistent reports that your mind will begin to accept and then integrate this most powerful life-altering truth.

When I sense that someone might be open to a bit more "out of the box" subject matter, I gently open the door to see if they want to go there. When they do, I often decide to be vulnerable enough to talk about personal experiences and then possibly about NDEs to open the doors that much wider. Most of the time, they are interested and maybe even inspired enough to do some reading later down the line. However, on rare occasions, I've experienced that since I was vulnerable enough to share, they have a sense that they can trust me enough be share their personal NDE or even one of a family member or friend. So far, I have personally talked to fourteen such people, one of the last being my father.

Additionally, I have read more than thirteen books on the subject as well as watched many hours of people on YouTube telling us what happened to them. They do so from their hearts. Out of compassion for the rest of us, they want to help us towards being liberated from the fear of death and acceptance that, from the growth of the soul point of view, there is always a beautiful purpose for everything we witness as well as for those who witness what we experience.

For those who have had such an event, and possibly for you, knowledge of this life-changing understanding is a major contribution towards experiencing a happier, more fulfilling and peaceful life.

Witnessing the additional agonizing unbearable intense suffering people experience without this understanding is one of the driving factors for me putting these words to paper.

As many of us have, I have experienced deep and excruciating personal tragedies. Even with the benefit of an elevated level of knowledge, confidence, and trust that all that comes to us is a gift, I still experienced intense emotional and mental pain.

The good news is that when I became conscious enough to remember what I am sharing with you now, it was like having a lifeline thrown to me just before I sank into the depths.

As an example; soon after dropping to my knees after learning of my 33 year old son's passing, I started searching for how there could be any positive purpose for his exit. It wasn't long until answers based on what I learned about NDE's started to drift into my mind. Those answers soothed my soul enough to regain the trust that there would be a light at the end of the tunnel, even if I had yet to perceive it. Each event in your life is for personal growth, be it difficult or fun.

Growth Opportunities

The way I understand the process, first nature gently knocks on our door, and if we don't respond, the knock will progressively get louder and more determined. If we are too lost in what we are doing to pay attention, nature will break the door down, shake the house, or find another way to get our attention. It is much more fun to respond to the soft knocking, at which time we can simply make subtle adjustments that change the course of our life. When on a long journey, adjusting one's course by just one degree on the compass will make a huge difference in where one ends up.

When we are really paying attention, we can learn much of what we came here for, while in a state of joyful fulfillment or what is also termed "coherence", so we don't need to depend upon disappointment or tragedy to bring us forward. Since we tend to be saturated with a culture focused on the negative, we tend to live in a state of incoherence, leading to layers of disappointment to overcome, and yet if we rise to the challenge, we are richer for the experience.

The end goal is always to reconnect with the truths that will bring us back into a state of joy. The more we look for the gift of love, the sooner we are lifted into peace.

If you were in a gym working out and experiencing the pain of the reps, you would still finish your set because you want the benefits. Likewise, you came to this gym called your life because you wanted to experience the mental, emotional, and spiritual strength gained through learning about commitment, discipline, understanding, acceptance, humility, and love.

Do You Want To Improve Your Life?

My words may ring a bell, but as mentioned before, they are not enough to sustain a change. If you are ready to make the effort to significantly improve the quality of your life, <u>make a decision now</u> to dedicate time to read about, or even better, listen to at least ten people who have had a near-death experience via YouTube.

My guess is that after reading just a book or two, or listening to just a few people on YouTube, instead of needing to push yourself, you will feel pulled to read or listen to many more such accounts. For your convenience, I have provided a few suggestions at the end of this booklet.

Each of us has a truth meter, and it is <u>so very important</u> to give it the respect it deserves. Once you learn to trust that meter, when it affirms that what you are receiving is true, you will find the opinions of others to have much less influence… unless of course, they are speaking of an even higher level of truth.

After you have experienced the general consistency of at least ten reports of NDEs, new truths will be anchored, and your life will be changed in a very positive way. It is that simple.

Please accept this gift to you from yourself. By doing so, you will have a greater sense of your true home and walk through the rest of your life with a more peaceful heart. Think about that for a moment. You have the opportunity right now to change the course of your life. Just pull up one NDE on YouTube and see if your interest is piqued. As your life improves, the world around you also benefits.

Expanding consciousness is not always comfortable, because we and our loved ones like the stability of sameness even though in reality, everything is always changing, or we would die of boredom.

Please be aware that some that are close will expand with you, and others will be stretched beyond their comfort zone, and therefore, you may drift apart. Will you forge ahead as an example of what is possible or try to remain within your joint comfort zone? Since you cannot "unknow" something, you will <u>already</u> have moved forward internally, but it might take a while to manifest externally. Even if you try to move back a step to make both of you feel more comfortable, by doing so, you will eventually start to resent each other. You because you are driven to freely express your truths and the other because, on some level, they will feel coddled and placated. So it is truly nobler to feel the space, enjoy the awakening, smile, and go on with child-like curiosity about what is next. By being the example, you help to set others free too.

What Are <u>You</u> Going To Do?

Believe it or not, at this very moment, the universe is presenting you with this information and asking you that question. What are you going to do?

It does not matter when these words were written or by whom. In a way, they were created by you for this very moment.

As you read these words, you are in the present moment of your life.

There are no accidents or coincidences. There is you, now.

All that comes to you is a gift to accept or reject. Please do not worry. You cannot get it wrong! This is your life, and everything that happens is to help you grow. If we scrape our knee, we learn how to be more careful. When we find a very special spot we like to visit, we remember where it is and how to get there again.

The fastest and easiest way to move forward at this moment is to go to YouTube and type in NDE or Near-Death Experiences. Sometimes you will get people who are referring to an event in which they narrowly missed being killed, as opposed to a true NDE, wherein one has medically died, gone up a tunnel into a light, visited with elevated beings, and returned, or something similar.

Some reports are shorter and more direct, and others have a longer story to tell. It takes more patience to listen to the longer reports; however, by doing so, you will have a greater sense of the truth of who that person is and, therefore, a greater opportunity for your truth meter to evaluate the authenticity. Each person's experience is via the filter of the culture they were raised in, so please focus on the amazing consistencies rather than getting lost in the differences of the filters. I know of what I speak.

You may feel as I did that you have finally found a source to quench an underlying thirst. Even when you are exposed to a new understanding that you recognize to be true, it is only through repetition that you will be able to rewire the well-established neuro-pathways creating your current foundational perceptions. For good reasons, it takes quite a bit of exposure to readjust our foundations. Otherwise, we would suffer from too much instability.

When listening to someone tell of their experience, trust your truth meter. If you feel that party has an agenda of manipulation, trust yourself and move on to the next one. I've only come across two who were doing that, which was disappointing until I went back into trust with the understanding that everything has its purpose, and sometimes the purpose is to create a contrast of one against the other to test and anchor what is real.

Perception

Each decision you make stands on its own, and the repercussion of each decision depends on how each is perceived by yourself and others.

It is in your ability to perceive that you have the greatest capacity for growth and good health. Do you see the glass half empty or half full? Have the events of your life been a gift or a curse?

According to research done by biologist Bruce Lipton (go to YouTube, he is a treasure), the way you perceive life actually changes the way your genes express the chemical information that affects your quality of mental, emotional and physical health.

If you completely trusted a mentor such as a spiritual being or someone like Merlin, Yoda, Padme, Obi-Wan Kenobi, Meera, etc., when they assigned a task for you to complete, even if you didn't want to do it, you would know that they did so out of love and for the benefit of your growth.

Just as often depicted, the apprentice's mind will almost certainly fight doing as directed, which the mentor well knows. It is in the taming of the unruly, headstrong, wild horse within us, that we make the greatest progress. Feeling that uncomfortable fight means you are growing a new tooth of wisdom. Be kind, patient, and soothing with yourself; it is just a part of the process.

Think of the greater opportunities for experiencing the joy of progress when the energy of that horse becomes available to serve you instead of you serving it. How would that feel? Each horse you tame and integrate will increase your horsepower. 

You have, and always have had, access to your mentor (guide, guardian angel, or others who want to help), and that mentor energy has guided you to this very moment. Could that be true? Take a moment right now. Does some part of you recognize a glimmer of truth within that statement? What was the source of inspiration for you to read these words? What pulled you to continue to read this far?

What are you thinking? Does your thought help or hinder you? Are your thoughts leading you towards your goals?

Every decision we make is like coming to a fork in a river in which we need to decide which way we are going to choose. Those life force currents may merge back together just around the next bend, or they may lead to vastly different places.

The more tuned in we are, the sooner we will sense which one is best for us. As our 'internal guidance' kicks into gear, we eventually make the decision we were 'inspired' (in spirit) to make. 'Inspired' means we received 'divine breath' or 'divine guidance'.

Even if we make a last-minute, panicked decision, it was still in that last moment that we received the guidance to take us to where we will gain the most benefit for our soul's growth. No doubt, that internal voice just kept turning up the volume until we finally got the message.

What is more attractive to you, fighting the current and living life in a state of panic or going with the flow, seeing what is ahead of you, conserving energy, and having the time to perceive a purpose in the direction you feel compelled to choose?

What is more attractive to you? That simple question turns out to be quite profound, yet one of the least asked questions, and therefore, one of the least answered.

The first step is to ask something like, "How can I live life with greater ease and a greater sense of unfolding purpose?"

The asking creates a void, and nature always seeks to fill a void, so after asking, the next step is learning to quiet one's mind enough to listen. The answer may come right away or gradually sneak up on you over time. Either way, I love feeling that 'Ah-ha!' moment as the answer appears. Is it 'just' your imagination providing answers, or does the universe communicate to us through our imagination? I think it's the latter.

Listening to and acting upon what you perceive to be your internal inspired guidance does not guarantee you will have the desired outcome. You are only guaranteed that whatever unfolds will be orchestrated to better prepare you for what lies ahead. IF you can truly trust that such is the case, then all forms of fear fade away, and peace of heart reigns. Are you ready? Quiet your mind, ask, be open to receiving, act on inspiration, and trust life IS happening FOR you, rather than TO you. Check out NDEs and change the course of your life.

Control

We all want more control over every aspect of our lives and others' lives for both altruistic and selfish reasons. It is our nature to do so, and therefore, we will, of course, experience others wanting to control us in one way or another, directly or indirectly, through subtle or gross manipulation.

When you feel another 'trying' to convince you to change your mind about something, most of the time there are two primary reasons; 1, they believe it is best for you to do so, and 2, because if they are successful, they will feel more secure about their own beliefs. A sincere agreement will shore up their doubts, while an insincere agreement will just frustrate both of you. Feeling resistant to what they offer can indicate that there is some truth being offered that you have yet to accept, or it could be that it is time to let go of that relationship for the time being.

A way to move out of possible conflict is to trust that there is always some gift to be gained from what the universe has expressed to you. If you are conscious enough to consider that possibility, you can simply smile and sincerely say, "Thank you for sharing your thoughts, and I will consider what you have offered," or something to that effect. By doing so, you will have added to their sense of worth and enhanced your own.

Reacting to such an event with negative emotion lowers your frequency, and you can feel the difference. Every time you catch yourself and change your perception, you are letting old neural pathways (habits) fade while reinforcing new neural pathways towards a better life.

Words are very powerful because they are essentially keystrokes that activate subconscious programing. For instance, if you say, "This stress is killing me," you set programs in motion to give you what you've asked for. Alternatively, you can switch your internal or external comment to, "This stress is great because I know that these challenges are helping me to enhance my capacity, strength, and wisdom."

Which outcome are you more attracted to, creating self-destruction or self-improvement? There is hard science backing up what I have just implied here. (check out Bruce Lipton)

You can find tremendous support for improving yourself through different forms of creating new neural pathways and new ways of thinking that change how your life unfolds on YouTube via Marisa Peer, Fearless Soul, Bruce Lipton, Joe Dispenza, Vishen Lakianie, Tom Bilyeu interview of Joe Dispenza, as well as others you can access if search "neural plasticity", etc.

Our ability to heal ourselves is taking a dramatic turn through many venues. Most recently, I have been fully engaged with the work of Dr. Joe Dispenza, and as with the NDEs, if you will take thirty minutes of your life to watch two or three Joe Dispenza Testimonials on YouTube, I guarantee you will be shocked and incredibly intrigued by what is being accomplished.

Lastly, please consider watching a movie on Amazon titled "Superhuman; The invisible becomes visible".

Would you believe normal children are taught to read or play vigorous physical games with thick blindfolds on? We live in an expanding, very dynamic, world, and that movie will help you grasp that we have so much more capacity than we've been led to believe. You may wonder how it could be that this level of human experience is still so buried followed by, wondering what else is openly out there but unknown by the masses?

Gratitude To Who?

When you find yourself feeling deep gratitude for a special moment in your life, like seeing a stunning sunset, snowcapped mountains, beautiful flowers, fall colors, beautiful reflections on water, a newborn child or animal, or just realizing how lucky you are to have a really good friend, etc., to whom or what are feeling grateful towards?

Please take a moment right now to remember feeling that way and consider the simple yet powerful connection to something greater than yourself that you experienced. We tend to let those moments drift away like steam off a hot drink instead of recognizing the truth of who we are and our two-way connection to the very source of our life energy. What are you grateful for right now? Feel it and explore it.

LIFEFORCE – SON, JOHN.

What is the difference between something alive and something dead?

The life force is there, and then it is not.

The energy pulsing through each cell of your body is the animating force that may be called your soul energy. There are many other ways to refer to that force, such as 'source', 'universal life energy', 'energy impulses', etc. All are appropriate.

What comes next is more about a very personal event regarding my son John. I am sharing it with you to provide an example of one of the many experiences I, and millions of others, have had in some form or another.

John had a successful business and was seemingly very in love with his wife, his two beautiful children, and their many friends; however, he left his body early one morning, by his hand, at the age of thirty-three.

As you can well imagine, hearing of his death was a 'drop to my knees' moment like no other in my life. If I had not had the grace of studying NDEs, I might not have made it through one of the two most difficult days in my life.

Later that day, while I was driving home from my daughter-in law's house by myself and crying out loud in intense grief, all of a sudden, John came into my mind and said, "Dad, since you believe in the continuum of life, I want to help you. First of all, never hold back grief because it is a part of the healing process." Then he said, "I want you to think of a time that you were gazing at me and simply being in love with me."

I did so, and he could tell I was there. He then said, "What I want you to realize is that what you were so in love with was the soul energy radiating out of my body. Our relationship has not ended; it has just changed."

I immediately responded out loud, "Thank you, John, that helps."

All I can tell you is that I know the difference between my mental musings and my son communicating with me.

There is much more to share in that regard, but I've already done so in my previous book, 'Some of What I've Learned So Far'. The point of sharing this much right now is to provide you with the opportunity to open yourself to a greater understanding and to challenge you to trust your inner 'truth meter'.

Did I just share a truth with you? Was I sharing a very real event, the acceptance of which may change your life, or was it a fantasy I imagined to help me feel better about what happened?

What does your gut, heart, truth meter tell you?

Truth Meter

What does your truth meter tell you, and can you trust it?

How much practice have you had? You have been in training since you were around seven or eight years old.

Between conception and seven or eight, we are just dry sponges indiscriminately soaking up whatever water we are exposed to, regardless of the quality. That is how we pick up a language and how we learn to live within a given culture. After seven or eight, we start to develop our capacity to question what is real and what is not.

Since you were essentially pre-programmed in your early years, most of your responses to life are based on those subconscious learned behaviors instead of your own conscious judgments of what is real, fair, and right. Your programing was/is continually reinforced in many ways through your family, their culturally aligned friends, and their culturally aligned children.

Allowing yourself the freedom to have a different perspective has, and probably still does, require a great deal of courage. Be courageous and yet be kind about how you do so. Sometimes, the energy it takes to break out of the box we've contained ourselves in can cause unintended collateral damage.

Acceptance of the feedback from your truth meter has been the key to discovering your independence, and we have all experienced that phenomenon. I am referring to the moment when you started to question what you were trained to accept.

Sometimes, if we conclude that we were not given the known truth, even if it was for 'our own good', it can be very upsetting to the very foundation we built our life upon. For instance, if Santa is not real, what other surprises are coming our way? Maybe there is some segment of our population that we've been programmed to despise or look down upon that we now (hopefully) realize are just as worthy as anyone else?

We are all subject to the group consciousness passed on through the programming from the previous generations because it started happening in the womb.

Your parents raised you before they had much chance to personally evolve, so how could they pass on anything other than how they were programmed plus whatever truths they may have been able to integrate by then. If you are a parent, you have, and are, doing the same thing, to one degree or another, even if you think otherwise.

Like our parents, we do not like our teenagers to react or be judgmental with us, however it almost certainly does happen because that awkward time is a part of nature. If the parents are exceptionally controlling, the reactions may not happen until later, but, in most cases, they will come to pass, obvious or not.

In those early years, young people are no longer comfortable within the protective cocoon of truths their parents wove for them based on their interpretation of the world. Teenagers are in the process of discovering what is true for them. Those protective walls have now become restrictive barriers causing a claustrophobic response that demand strong action just to be able to breathe and regain a feeling of freedom of movement.

Each generation thinks (and rightly so) that they are doing a better job than their parents did, so they believe they and their child will be spared the struggle. The societal and technical realities facing any teenager are so vastly different from their parents' realities at that same age that it is impossible for a parent to truly grasp what their child is experiencing.

The more a parent accepts this aspect of nature and encourages their child to discover their own truths, the more likely they will accept their parent as a distant, or maybe even close, ally.

Your truth meter allowed you to become an independent thinker, and it is one of the most valuable assets you have, yet most of us do not give it the credit it deserves.

Have you observed people without the benefit of a well-developed truth meter trying to navigate life's challenges?

Some may have lost trust in their ability to sense what is best because of the failures that come from using our truth meter as a divining rod to help win at something like picking a stock or some form of gambling. They may have sensed their power to discern truth but were not trained how and when to use it, as I can personally attest to.

I am seventy, and I am still learning how to trust my truth meter and navigate life.

Growing Pains

As your consciousness heightens, from that elevated perspective you will become aware of truths that others have yet to realize. If you mention or imply your awareness of one of those truths to another, since we all tend to resist change, their reaction may seem like an effort to suppress your thinking. However, due to their being in the same programing you were subject to, they, like you, will resist new information because it _is_ disruptive to the comfort of their foundation. In such a moment, we can choose to give in to feeling resentment and anger towards such a person for being stuck in a lower frequency in their patterning, or alternatively, to be grateful for the elevated consciousness gained while having compassion for those who have yet to experience the view from your new perspective. How silly would it be for a fifth-grader to be upset with a fourth-grader for not knowing fifth-grade material?

So please keep in mind that whenever <u>you</u> are feeling resistant, it might be because you are exposed to yet another level of truth that disrupts your foundation's security.

It seems that a part of our evolutionary progress is to suffer through the consequences of the feelings and expression of anger directly or indirectly, both to us and from us, which are hurtful whether expressed from us or to us.

From your side, once you become conscious of your unconscious angry outburst or otherwise communicated negative emotion (like a nasty glance etc.), immediately apologizing is very healing. The humility of apologizing right away tends to become etched into our history in a way that will make it easier to remember to be more conscious and compassionate the next time. The longer you take to apologize, the more difficult it becomes, and yet it is then more important to do for your sake and theirs.

When you are on the other end of that same stick, as will often be the case, rather than reacting to a reaction, please consider the possibility that there is a gift for you, even if it was delivered out of frustration.

We all want to be heard and have our perspectives validated. For most of us, it takes a while to build up the courage to express ourselves. So when another is building their courage to express something to us, there are at least two pressure points. One pressure point is from being frustrated with themselves for holding back, and the second is the frustration we feel regarding something you did or did not do. Consequently, there is often an awkward emotional outburst. We all know what that is about.

Do yourself the favor of making an earnest inquiry regarding their perspective, which will serve to validate the other, and very often, you will gain some benefit as well. Validating another's process does not need to mean that you agree with them. You can simply say thank you for having the courage to share your perspective.

If you don't know it, there is an art to living. Please trust that you will keep getting better and better at it for as long as you are here. Each growth opportunity provides more insights for you to raise your awareness. As said previously, each step up provides you with a higher perspective, and when you see more of the big picture, it is easier to navigate a more peaceful way forward.

Access To Helpers

We have all heard of Carnegie Hall. How is Andrew Carnegie relevant? He was one of the richest men in America, and he knew about and utilized certain secrets to success that had been closely held by only the very wealthy of the world for many generations. He felt it was time for those secrets to be shared with the masses and eventually found the right guy to help him in a young man named Napoleon Hill. He shared with Napoleon the existence of angelic type 'helpers' and many other wonderful insights. Napoleon incorporated Andrew's guidance, and to his astonishment, he kept compounding his successes. Eventually, Napoleon compiled what he learned from his magnificent mentor in a book he wrote titled 'Think and Grow Rich'.

Many of Andrew's contemporaries, like the Fords and the Edisons, were influential and successful people in the world at that time. They knew about, utilized, and attributed their successes to these secret truths and supported Andrew's goal by allowing themselves to be interviewed by Napoleon.

'Think and Grow Rich' was published in 1937 and was a worldwide bestseller for eighty years, so the idea of there being loving, supportive resources to access beyond our conscious awareness is by no means new, or limited to "new age" people, although it may be new to you.

If it is new to you, allow yourself to have the humility to accept that the timing has not been right for you until now (I've had that experience many times) and have gratitude for this moment.

Throughout the existence of humanity, there have always been those who, due to experiencing a profound personal awakening of some sort, were compelled to share what they learned, and therefore they became speakers, authors, religious leaders, spiritual teachers, etc. Out of compassion, they wanted others to know of the life-altering truths they were exposed to.

The point is that, for many people, these concepts are as normal as apple pie and are critical to their happiness and a sense of purpose.

You stayed with what I have offered so far because you are a seeker of greater truths. You know you are actively improving your life and the lives of your loved ones and I deeply appreciate you are doing so.

Reading 'Think and Grow Rich' and other similar offerings will definitely, and very tangibly, improve your life. Even though Napoleon's writings are based on the insights of absolute pillars of society, those profound life-altering insights are not taught in public schools. We are a rigid society, and change has been slow. I would guess that most of those who have read Think and Grow Rich have not made the effort to get their children and grandchildren engaged, for fear of loss of being identified as a rational being.

How much longer do you think you will live?

If it is going to be quite a while, you may as well continue to do as much as you can to make the journey as enjoyable as possible.

Become An Active Seeker Of Truth

Just like in a digital game, each new truth you discover will give you more 'life energy', although that 'life energy' will be much more rewarding. Sometimes, one truth will replace another because we are ready for the 'next level' of growth. Most of the time, new truths re-shape and strengthen our foundation while affirming our deepest connection to the source from which we came.

Experiencing good health and wellbeing has everything to do with trusting that <u>you are unconditionally loved, and all that unfolds before you is for a beautiful purpose</u>. Everything you experience is a gift to help you grow in every way and especially spiritually, be it fun, or a challenge. The more effort you exert looking for the gifts, the more you will recognize them, and over time you will gain more appreciation for the value and the timing of each one.

Old habit patterns are strong, so sometimes, our minds will challenge us with doubts about our conclusions. Each time you re-evaluate and reaffirm what you know to be true, you strengthen your foundation and increase your 'life energy'. Wrestling with your mind can be very challenging, like making a new path through untamed foliage; however, with each effort, the path becomes more worn and easier to traverse.

Sometimes, when a really big challenge is upon me, I've had to ask myself, "What do you really believe?" I then say to myself, "OK, let's go back to the most basic bricks in my foundation to reaffirm what is real for me. It takes some time to do so and it is always very helpful."

At the opposite end of that spectrum is living as though everything is a burden, which stimulates; stress, anxiety, anger, sadness, depression, etc., depleting your 'life energy' spawning illness and misery.

How can you transition from fear's disruptive and destructive elements towards the uplifting and rejuvenating elements of trust?

To start with, please trust that you were attracted to read this booklet for some good reason. If you act on what you've gained, the benefits of doing so will serve you for the rest of your life.

Go to YouTube and listen to one of the most current cutting-edge biologists named Bruce Lipton. He is an excellent and very engaging teacher who will help you understand in simple terms that how we perceive the world changes the chemistry that builds or destroys our bodies. You will love what you learn and want to share it with others.

Next, listen to some of Dr. Joe Dispenza's testimonials because they are so profound that you will want to know more about how these seeming miraculous, yet scientifically developed, events can occur.

You will almost certainly know of someone you will think of who could benefit from his work. His extensive personal experience and twenty years of research have led him to wonderful life-changing insights you may want to integrate into your life.

Bruce and Joe are very good friends, and both offer information backed up by in-depth scientific research, which will also help you understand how to move beyond the past habit patterns controlling your life much more than you would think. We don't know what we don't know.

Vishen Lakhiani of 'Mindvalley' is another tremendous resource, as is Marisa Peer and many others he collaborates with.

Wim Hof is yet another resource who has changed the medical world in a very empowering way. I've also been very impressed with my experience with Spring Forest Qigong, who has had some amazing success documented through the Mayo Clinic.

One last suggestion, watch "Superhuman; the invisible becomes visible" on Amazon. You will witness mind-expanding technology going on for twenty-plus years that many would not imagine possible, including normal children who have been taught to see while wearing very effective blindfolds. In addition, of course, blind people are also being taught how to see utilizing the same innate, yet untapped, abilities we all have. How? Watch the show!

If you take the time to listen to those who have had NDEs along with some or all of the people I've mentioned, you will gain insights that will change the course of your life in a very positive way. Changing your life today is changing your life forever. It is never an 'all or nothing' mandate. Take in what you can at this moment, don't worry about remembering the details, and just let it soak in by osmosis.

Having a deeper, much more grounded understanding of the dynamics of how your body works is foundational for further progress of your physical, emotional, mental, and spiritual wellbeing.

If you choose to commit to taking the time and effort to follow these few suggestions, you will come to accept and trust that everything in your life is unfolding for your benefit, even when it is not apparent to you. Doing so will dramatically expand your sense of peace, which stimulates the flow of inspiration and creativity.

To gain the level of trust I am referring to, I can't overstate the importance of studying NDEs, and the more, the better. Each account will fortify your new foundation based entirely upon what YOU recognize, at the deepest level, to be unwavering truths.

The greater the trust, the easier it will be for you to recognize and utilize the gifts being bestowed upon you.

As the frequency you are operating at increases, you will find yourself becoming more aware of certain colors for the first time, hearing a gentle breeze blowing through a tree, or birds singing in the distance. What feels so very nice in those moments is the heightened sense of your true nature and your connection to the source from which you came.

How has this information altered my life?

I grew in my capacity for love, empathy, and compassion due to my exposure to NDE's, which allowed me to survive the suicide death of my thirty-three-year-old son. As a result, I knew that 'he' had not ended. I knew that he arrived 'on time', and I knew that the agony and grief all of us who loved him would force spiritual growth for each that could not have happened in any other way.

Initially, my wife and I were repulsed by even the thought of going back to the beach, where he terminated the physical existence we knew as our son John Buck. Based on what I/we learned by studying NDE's, we realized that place was where he launched into pure spirit and had a profound merging into a love far greater than what we can imagine. That realization was so life-changing that we felt really good about taking flowers there to celebrate his transition into that light and love.

I maneuvered a big piece of driftwood down to the water; we loaded it with flowers, some beer, some 'beer bread' that he loved, and we launched it into the tidal waters. Each year we did so, the tears progressively transformed into warm-hearted smiles for the incredible gift we had in his physical state and the spiritual connection we enjoy now.

It is completely due to my exposure to NDEs that I could accept the opportunity and challenge to grow my soul. Just like experiencing muscles gained through the pain of lifting weights, so will you sense the deepening emotional, mental, and spiritual strength gained as one lives through the challenges of life.

The idea of calling such an event a blessing could create a negative reaction in some; however, as I've learned, everything that happens is a blessing; only our resistance binds us to a darker, dense and more painful life.

You will find that when you allow for the possibility of there being a good purpose for some sad or disappointing event, your mind will immediately start to imagine how that could be. As those ideas build and multiply, you will find yourself feeling better and better. As one feels better, one is much more likely to help another, even if it is just by the nature of our very presence.

I am someone who has always been empathic, as my father and grandfather, my eyes almost always water at touching moments. I feel others' suffering, and I also experience their joys. I loved my son with all my heart and suffered tremendously deep grief. What I've just shared is a result of many tears, questioning, listening, questioning again, and reaffirming the truths I've accepted, which always takes me back into trust, peace, and love. I was inspired to focus on the gift of what I had now instead of focusing on the dark empty space of loss. I have refocused on how incredibly fortunate I am to have had the privilege of having that soul in his physical form in my life for all those years and gratitude for the elevation I've experienced as a result of his transition.

It feels much better to live in gratitude and worse to be angry, resentful, or even just disappointed. Either perspective has value due to the growth gained. Feeling pain is nature's way of getting us to change what we are doing until we feel better. The feelings of joy, love, and wonder are nature's way of encouraging us in a more productive direction.

Please stay with me on this next one.

While leaving the full force of your healthy skeptic nature intact, be open enough to view some of the amazing 'mediums' like 'The Long Island Medium' or the 'Hollywood Medium'. There is much for you to gain by witnessing quality mediums astound those they are helping by mentioning information that no one else could have known about. Once that level of credibility has been firmly established, the medium can impart information from the subject's loved one that is vital to their long-term happiness. No matter how skeptical the party benefiting from that information might have been, you will witness and know in your heart that you just witnessed a shift in their consciousness, which will also create a shift in yours. See if you can find past episodes of 'The Long Island Medium'. While she is very sincere, she is also a loud, fun-loving human being, so her initial impression may not meet your expectations. Just stick with it for an episode or two; you won't be disappointed.

My wife and I experienced working with a medium that definitely altered our lives as well as others we shared our experience with. I have nothing to gain and lots of credibility to lose by sharing this with you, so I am not doing it lightly. Like you, I am a smart, skeptical, truth-seeking human being, so keep an open mind. In doing so, you might make similar conclusions, and if not, then you will at least have a great understanding of what others believe they have experienced.

I have already expressed what happened when my son first communicated with me the day he passed.

"Our relationship has not ended; it has just changed."

The Dragonfly

My wife and I had watched many episodes of the reality show called the Long Island Medium and demonstrations of mediums on popular talk shows. Since we both felt very connected to our son, we did not feel we needed to reach out to a medium; however, we did talk about the possibility and wondered if we should do so.

A month and a half or two after John's transition, John came into my head and said, "Find a medium, any medium." I told Jane this and, since I was very busy with work, I suggested that she start making some calls to friends to see if anyone had a good connection they could refer us to.

We were guided to a medium named Lynn Austin, who, at the time, lived in Colorado, and therefore, we talked with her over the telephone. We both agreed that our first meeting with her was the most powerful experience since the birth of our children. The shared sense of connection combined with the subtle nuances was way beyond what might otherwise be considered a hopeful imagination.

All communication with her has been over the telephone. Towards the end of our third meeting with her, she stated that John said to pay attention to dragonflies. We looked at each other puzzled, each shrugging our shoulders because neither of us had a point of reference associated with dragonflies.

Three days later, Jane was waiting for our seven-year-old grandson to meet her at the health club so she could take him swimming. He would walk from the grade school, about half a mile away, and when he got within sight of his grandmother, he would run to greet her with a big delicious hug. That day, when he walked out of the grade school, a big blue dragonfly landed on the top of his knuckles and stayed there until he arrived in front of Jane. As she could see him approaching, she was surprised that he did not break into his normal run, and then, as he got closer, she could perceive what was happening. She was inspired (thank you, John) to pull out her camera and take a picture, after which the dragonfly flew away. Out of respect for his mother, who had different perspectives at the time, Jane simply said, "Whenever I see a dragonfly, I think of your dad."

I carry that picture with me always. Whenever I feel inspired to share that experience with someone, I show them that picture. Upon doing so, I almost always note a profound acceptance of the reality I just shared with them and can almost feel the reverberations impacting their lives due to doing so. That precious gift has shifted the consciousness of many lives.

Could it have been a coincidence? What do you think?

I know this; I have no memory of ever witnessing a dragonfly landing on me or anyone else for more than a second or two, if at all.

I accept that for a dragonfly to stay on the hand of a seven-year-old boy for around fifteen minutes, three days after being told to "Pay attention to dragonflies," as profound evidence of the connections that exist between here and there.

Additional events confirm our connection with John that have made us smile, feel warm, and sometimes tear up. Each one has reinforced that our relationship is a continuum and that we will continue to walk this path together while we are here and as we transition to there.

A broken heart is also a heart that has been broken open. The key to surviving the challenge of making it through such intense pain is to accept that it is a forced growth spurt that we needed and probably previously and collectively agreed upon.

It is one thing to sign up for a tough educational course and quite another to do the work. Our life is a magnificent collaboration with those here and there, all of which is meant to help us expand our capacity to 'know' love.

A Serious Health Challenge

In December 2015, I was diagnosed with squamous cell carcinoma via a biopsy of a growth in my throat that looked like a swollen tonsil.

As a result of my exposure to NDEs, I accepted that diagnosis with an open heart and zero dread or fear. I had learned and accepted that everything happens for a very good reason. I knew that the essence of who I am is the animating life force within me called my soul, that my purpose for being here was to grow, and that I would learn a lot from this experience. I also sensed that another purpose for the cancer was to prepare me to help others in need, and that has certainly been the case.

I went from being late stage 4, very close to dying within a few months, to having a dramatic turnaround within just three weeks at an alternative hospital in Tijuana, Mexico, called CHIPSA. Ninety-five percent eventually disappeared, but that last 5% started to grow again about six months later at a much more aggressive rate, so by January 2021, I was told that I had around thirty days to live.

Along the way, I had to decide what direction to take, surgery, radiation, and chemo, or go with non-toxic alternative solutions.

Fortunately, I was already very aware of many successes in healing even stage 4 cancers with non-toxic approaches, the knowledge of which contributed greatly to my rather calm response to my diagnosis. Additionally, I had learned to be fairly confident with my internal guidance. I tap into that guidance to approach serious decisions via sensing either a red, yellow, or green light. Red means stop, yellow means caution, and green means go. If I did not get a green light, I didn't 'go', even when there was the pressure of many valid personalities and reasons for doing so.

For example, the following is an event that happened at least eight months before going to CHIPSA. From the Ear Nose Throat surgeon's point of view, it looked like there was no hope left, so he gave me a very intense recommendation to have a tracheotomy. He said that it would be with me for the rest of my life (which I know he did not think would be that long), and if I did not do so, I would be exposing my wife to witness a horrible and fatal event. He stated that it was his firm belief that I would very likely die while choking and gasping for air unless I could pull the plug on the tracheotomy to start breathing again through that hole. My wife was very concerned, and I certainly did not want to expose her to that kind of trauma, so I gave very heavyweight to his recommendations. Since no matter how hard I tried, I could not get an internal 'green light', I said no to the tracheotomy for now and that I would continue to consider what he had said.

As another example, two weeks before I went to CHIPSA, the pain had increased to the point that I went to the emergency room at the small local hospital in the middle of the night. I wanted them to lance the bottom of the tumor to allow it to drain and relieve the pressure causing the intense pain. I was treated very kindly and with considerable feelings of urgency and compassion, but they said they were not in a position to help me. They wanted to give me morphine for the pain and highly recommended that I allow them to fly me to a major hospital in Seattle. They also expressed that if I went, I should be prepared to follow that hospital's recommendations, one of which would certainly be a tracheotomy.

I associated morphine with an 'end of life' scenario, so I rejected that offer, even though at this point it was looking pretty grim with little hope for a turnaround. I seriously considered their recommendations for myself and my wife's benefit, but even with that level of intense urgency, I could not get a green light. I remembered that I had some leftover painkillers from a dentist that I had not used up and that I had a salve that might quickly burn a hole that would allow drainage and relieve the pressure. Since I had practiced learning to listen to my internal voice, I trusted the guidance always available, and we went home. The painkillers temporarily gave me greatly appreciated relief.

Within thirty-six hours, the salve opened a hole that released the fluid that was building up, and with that pressure relieved, I was able to switch to ibuprofen. Now that I could focus again, I started re-examining the tools I had to see if any stronger applications might elicit the response I so desperately needed.

Five or six days before going to the emergency room, through the guidance of a trusted therapist, I had a personal spiritual experience. That experience of profound connection affirmed to me that I had finally learned what I needed to learn from the cancer and therefore I was now on my way to recovery.

Within a week of my visit to the emergency room, my wife saw a before and after picture of a man that demonstrated a 95% reduction of a humungous tumor three times the size of mine within just eight weeks with no surgery or radiation and with only very light (10%) doses of chemo. He had gone to the CHIPSA Hospital, so I called them, and they said that the last fifteen or twenty cases of my type of cancer had met with great success.

I had already drained our financial resources and created significant debt during the three years and eight months I had been dealing with this issue, so I did not have the money to go there. I was offered a loan from my angelic mother, which I saw as a blessing to proceed. Ten days later, I was at CHIPSA starting treatment, and three weeks later, 65% of the cancer had melted away. A little over three months after my return from CHIPSA, the cancer has been reduced by the 95%.

As stated, about sixteen months later, I found myself even closer to leaving this world. I was told I probably had less than 30 days to live, which made sense to me as I could see the cancer growing on a week-by-week basis, closing my throat to the point that it was kind of like trying to breathe through a straw. Fortunately, the doctors at CHIPSA came up with a new plan that worked very fast with the assistance of three acupuncture treatments per week from an unaffiliated doctor down the street. In 12 days, I could see no more cancer in my throat. There were still areas I couldn't see, but it was also diminishing quickly. The result is that I was given the 'all clear' from a top Earn Nose & Throat Surgeon at the University of Washington about five months later.

The way I see it, having cancer is what I needed to help my soul grow, so it will be a win for my soul no matter what the eventual outcome is. Each time I've been able to really "get that", I become relaxed and full of trust, which is a wonderful way to live.

When I think about those who have gone through such circumstances without assimilating these truths, I feel great empathy and compassion. I give deep thanks to God for the grace that allowed me to have the perspective I do, without which, the pain, suffering, and fear would be ten times what mine has been.

Where's the end of you and the beginning of God? Is there a boundary line? When we are inspired to do something, we are 'in spirit'. Did I have a choice about writing if I was inspired to do so?

I believe God's empathy and compassion for all suffering souls has been the genesis for the inspiration to write these words. If just one person finds some relief, I will be very pleased to have had that tiny, yet maybe transformative, role to play in their lives.

You are an amazing human being. How do I know that? You made it this far, and only an amazing human being seeking after truth would have done so.

Thank you. I appreciate you, and I wish you the very best in all ways possible. Peace and love be with you always.

– Sam Buck

www.ingramcontent.com/pod-product-compliance
Lightning Source LLC
Chambersburg PA
CBHW061709130726
47996CB00006B/2222